Monster Poems

Compiled by John Foster

Contents

Acknowledgements

The Editor and Publisher wish to thank the following who have kindly given permission for the use of copyright material:

Finola Akister for Who's Ugly? © Finola Akister 1991; Tony Bradman for Monsters and Leave the whales alone, please both © Tony Bradman 1991; Eric Finney for IT © Eric Finney 1991; Theresa Heine for The mermaid © Theresa Heine 1991; Wendy Larmont for Happynessy © Wendy Larmont 1991; Charles Thomson for The lost mermaid and The sea-monster's snack both © Charles Thomson 1991; Clive Webster for Meal-time © Clive Webster 1991.

Although every effort has been made to contact the owners of copyright material, a few have been impossible to trace, but if they contact the Publisher, correct acknowledgement will be made in future editions.

Printed in Hong Kong

Monstros

Down at the bottom
Of the deep blue sea
There's lots of things
That we can't see.

There might be monsters
Down in the deep
That would give you nightmares,
Ruin your sleep.

There might be horrors
Lurking below . . .
And if there are
I don't want to know!

Tony Bradman

3

Meal-time

The octopus has got eight arms,
And I just cannot see
Which ones he uses to eat food
When he sits down to tea.

Does he have four knives and forks?
It really is amusing.
I wonder how he hits his mouth –
It must be quite confusing.

Clive Webster

The sea-serpent

A sea-serpent saw a big tanker,
Bit a hole in her side and then sank her.
It swallowed the crew
In a minute or two,
And then picked its teeth with the anchor.

Anon

5

The sea-monster's snack

Deep down upon his sandy bed
the monster turned his slimy head,
grinned and licked his salty lips
and ate another bag of ships.

Charles Thomson

Happynessy

Monster Nessy in the Loch,
Sleeps inside a cave of rock.
She swims around and round all day.
It seems a lonely way to play.

So when the tourists stand and stare
She pops her head up in the air.
They gasp and take a photograph,
And monster Nessie starts to laugh.

She quickly dives and hides below.
Is she real? They'll never know!

Wendy Larmont

IT

It was huge,
It was enormous,
It came dripping from the sea;
It wobbled down the promenade,
It passed quite close to me!

It ruined all the flower-beds,
It upset an ice-cream stall,
It was like a giant jelly-fish and
It had no eyes at all.

It cleared the paddling pool of kids,
Its feelers swung and swayed,
It seemed to like the fruit machines as
It oozed through the arcade.

It burst the turnstile on the pier as
It squeezed its green mass through,
It left a horrid track behind –
It was like a trail of glue.

It reached the pier's end railings and
It forced them till they split.
It flopped back down into the sea and
It vanished. That was It.

Eric Finney

9

Who's ugly?

The monster was big, he was ugly,
He lived in the deeps of the sea.
He had three different eyes, but only one ear,
And a mouth where his chin ought to be.

He was covered with seaweed and shells
But he wasn't too bothered with those.
He had twenty two legs, twenty two feet,
And a bump on the end of his nose.

It's quite sad to say he was made in this way,
For this monster was loving and kind.
And when fish in the sea went out for their tea
They left him their babies to mind.

There's a moral, of course, to this story,
So remember, for what it is worth,
That your goldfish might think when you watch him,
That you're the ugliest person on earth.

Finola Akister

Leave the whales alone, please!

Leave the whales alone, please,
They don't do any wrong;
They swim in every ocean,
And fill them with their songs.

Leave the whales alone, please,
Like us, they've got a brain;
But if we don't start using ours,
We won't see them again.

Leave the whales alone, please,
We need them in the seas;
We need their life and beauty,
And all they need is peace.

Leave the whales alone, please,
Let them live their lives,
Let them leap, and swim, and sing –
Let the whales survive!

Tony Bradman

13

The mermaid

A mermaid sat
On a sandy rock,
And her eyes gleamed soft and green,
'Come with me,' she called,
'And I'll take you away
To the land beneath the sea.'

'We'll ride on a dolphin,
We'll tickle a whale,
Eat seaweed cake for our tea,'
And she held out her hand
As she dived through the waves,
'Come with me
        Come with me
                Come with me.'

Theresa Heine

The lost mermaid

A mermaid came out of the plug hole
And said with a frown, 'Excuse me,
I think I have made a wrong turning.
Is this a cave in the sea?'

Charles Thomson